YET STILL WE KNEEL

Yet Still We Kneel

J. H. McCandless

with drawings by
GERARD **NEGELSPACH**

The Hemlock Press
Alburtis, Pennsylvania

Printed and published by The Hemlock Press
Rural Delivery, Alburtis, Pennsylvania 18011

this book is affectionately dedicated to
ALMIGHTY GOD
who took time out from a busy schedule
to invent, nurture, and discover to me my wife
DOROTHY MAHLE McCANDLESS
who is, I am firmly convinced, the only woman
who could have not only survived but flourished
under this difficult circumstance
and who has further borne us two sons
CHRISTOPHER and JOHN WOOLMAN
who had no choice in the matter
but have also managed admirably

"Variations on a Theme by John Donne" and "Letter to an American Advisor" were published in *The Christian Century* of Sept. 3, 1958, and March 31, 1965, respectively. "Lines for the Dedication of a Fallout Shelter" was published in the Oct. 12, 1962 issue of *Commonweal*. "Sonnet for My Thirty-fourth Birthday" and "For Wilmer Young" were published in *Friends Journal* of Sept. 13, 1958, and Aug. 22, 1959. "The Time Is Now Standard" first appeared in an issue of *Lehigh Valley Report,* a local anti-war bulletin published by William Wingell. "A Cross for Christmas" appeared in *The Pulpit* for December, 1962, published by The Christian Century Foundation. "Can These Bones Live?" was published in the Spring, 1962, issue of *Quaker Religious Thought*. I thank the editors of these publications for their encouragement.

The following poems have not been previously published: "Petition," "If I Forget Thee ...," "Ninth Hour," "Collage," "Never a Spray of Yew," "Reprise for Lewis Carroll," "And Smog." All other poems in this volume first appeared in the pages of *Approach: A Literary Quarterly*. It is difficult to express adequate appreciation for the stimulation and helpful criticism of the editors with whom I worked for twenty years: Helen Morgan Brooks, Carol Murphy, Sam Bradley, and most particularly the late Albert and Helen Fowler.

Also I want to record my gratitude to Mary Austin, Len and Mary Ann Cadwallader, Ginny Coover, Mickey Edgerton, Kathie and Pierce Hammond, Canby Jones, Geoff Kaiser, Dick and Phyllis Taylor, Rob and Cornelia Tucker, Mike and Margaret Yarrow, Mike and Ruth Yarrow, whose unexpected venture into "sharing the bread" has made possible the publication of this volume. How firmer than a Foundation ...

Petition

Bless me, Lord, as one who sits
    Steadfast, among the hypocrites.
If *their* prayers go up to thee
    — Perhaps there's hope for even me?

Yet Still We Kneel

YET STILL WE KNEEL

How Silently, How Silently...

Now God is born at evening, when each star
is visible, and makes the rounds of heaven
in harmony; no sun outshines the rest.
Motion, being evident and circular,
requires a center, more than earth or sun,
not finite — yet all finite things,
being part of this eternity, demand
to understand.   So Love reveals itself:
to these stars in their orbits, and to man
in star, child, manger, cross, and plan.

Having as all created things the power
to will disharmony and turn away,
break from his orbit like the meteor,
or, fruitless, multiply like cancered cells,
man faces outward from the silent core
of his true being, inwardly at war.
Now darkness falls, and still the silent stars,
swinging their wayward flocks across the sky
toward Bethlehem, look down and burn more bright
to light the coming of the Holy Child
that God and man may yet be reconciled.

Sonnet for My Thirty-fourth Birthday

Whether this life has not yet been required,
or, being required, is merely not yet given,
remains to be revealed. The law of heaven
allows us infinite delay: still unexpired,
God's statutes know no limitations, and we claim
postponements, prudence, compromise until
we make our own foreclosure to His will,
and serve ourselves the summons in His name.
We know not to what end we have been born,
nor of what truth our blood must be the seed;
we only know this time for which we plead
is ended when the cock's crow cries the morn.
. . . And then what justice shall my life afford,
that I have lived this year beyond my Lord?

Variations on a Theme by John Donne

Let not my mind be blinder by more light,
nor faith by reason added lose her sight.
Should darkness lift, let me not loose my guide,
for knowledge not yet deep may still be wide
and trackless; my uncertain circling stride
returns to darkness as the day to night.

Blind Saul knew only that the truth was bright
before truth's darkness fell and purified
the mind that knowledge had brought only pride,
the eyes that witnessed death and stood aside.
As he found vision with returning sight,
let not my mind be blinder by more light.

Let not vain thoughts to faithlessness invite;
nor mind's Creator be by mind denied.
Shall I, each day I meet Him crucified,
probe my reflective fingers in His side?
O let not sense join senses in their flight,
nor faith by reason added lose her sight.

Deliver, Lord, thy servant in his pride:
blind, open-eyed, sure, doubtful, narrow, wide,
free as the angels, to thy footstool tied
(where light is dim, and darkness glitters bright);
let not my mind be blinder by more light,
nor faith by reason added lose her sight.

If I Forget Thee...

To what strange land are these thy children come,
to hang hearts' harps on what square peg and weep?
by what strange discords lulled to joyless sleep?
led by what alien stars how far from home?

What blazing furnaces lie yet ahead?
what wasted cities wait us on the plain?
what hills will lift what burdens high again?
what rock shall roll thy children from the dead?

Lord, I will watch, though all the world should sleep,
though alien glitter make thy guidestar pale,
though faltering angels call thy fallen sheep,
though wiser men turn back, and shepherds fail.
Like Joseph by the manger, far from home,
Lord, I will sing, though all the world be dumb.

The Window

The sun comes up in the morning,
   and the sun goes down at night;
it carries a cautious warning
   on the subtleties of sight.

For the sun comes out of the ocean
   to shine on sages and fools;
yet its obvious westward motion
   is denied by the modern schools.

To the wise man it centers creation,
   and borders it to the dunce,
while mystical cerebration
   may see it both places at once.

And yet the sun, beyond surmise,
   obeys one certain rule:
to rise and shine upon the wise,
   and also on the fool.

This blessing then may wise men take,
   and fools for ever more;
and blessèd thrice be William Blake,
   who knew what eyes are for.

18

John Woolman

Bounded by contract, he takes up the pen
and writes the articles of sale — for men
must wear their tools until they fit no more —
signs, seals, delivers, shows them to the door,
and meets truth coming in.
                              Now God
will set the boundaries: benevolent neutrality
gives way to violent, inspired morality,
and old friends find him just, but somewhat odd.

The Jersey universe expands: he dreams of mines
across a sea of darkness, and declines
the business gambit; puts aside
encumbrance, superfluity, and pride;
consorts with slaves and masters, fears good friends are pained
that payment must be made where none seems due;
conquers his courage, seeks the savage too
("that haply some instruction may be gained")

and, sharing no tongue save truth, at journey's end
finds love's first motion makes the savage, friend.
     His will lies dead, slain by the twin sufficient swords
of faith and works; now God affords
for his soul's steerage: as he touches shore,
the sea-spent cock's crow greets the final isle

21

where death and smallpox wait; without denial
he trudges forward for one journey more.

God of the prophets, who took up the pen
the 'prentice hand let fall, now strike again:
and pierce our hearts that we may see
the Jersey shores of Galilee.

Can These Bones Live?

At least the furniture is familiar. Friends
being in all things non-essential slow to change
cling still to these rude benches, and arrange
benches and bones alike to fit the ends
of faded faith, and all the outworn gear
of men who talked with God within this hall.
Now these stone walls cry out for voices: all
is silence, and the speech is silence, here
where even silence once was speech, and stones could rest.

Restless, we probe the pottage of our souls,
finding no birthright, seeking to compose
disordered minds in primly ordered rows.
Not God, but peace and quiet are the goals,
and strength to bear our share of social sins
that man no longer shuns; to mitigate
the pain of our accepted low estate
with old, well-watered wine in modern skins,
and soothe the crying stone within each breast.

Now all is method, and there's magic in it:
technique to turn the times, or turn
us with the times. For us no bush will burn,
no voice invade the unconsuming minute
of our collected piety. Alone,
we worship our own shadows, and contrive

new platitudes to bring the dead alive,
ransack mankind to flesh the bleaching bone,
and find no power to save, or force to damn.

Afraid, we dare not strike the rock; events
dam up our thirst. Within these aging walls
we whistle, shaken reeds, against the squalls
of brutal time, and history's grim fence.
    Yet these walls speak, rebuking our dry bones
that rattle in whatever winds may blow
about the room. Be still. Let them cry out who know
that God may yet come down, and of these stones
raise up new children unto Abraham.

For Wilmer Young

Here am I, an old man in a dry courtroom,
trespasser at the seat of power, tester
of fears and fences, gate-scaler
in a world of wire, guards, checkpoints. I, grandfather
to a universe of climbing children, far from home:
yet not so far as you.

                       You say I turn the key,
imprisoning myself within those childless walls
and fences without progeny. Let it be so.

    Because I do not hope to climb
those many fences more. Because my age
is not for acrobatics, and my arms
will not support this weight of blood,
guilt, hatred, passion, men call *world*.

    I was a climber once: I hurdled pasture-fences,
scaled the sides of barns, and ran
through life and wheatfields. Now,
testing each foothold, painfully,
must climb the fences men erect
to hide their works from God.

                  O eagle-eyed young men,
did I amuse you as I crossed your fence?
Did wagers gauge my progress? Had my shirt been torn,
would you cast lots for souvenirs?

                  I have returned:

across your orchard-fence the apples are not edible.
Atop your gate I saw my prison walls, and turned the key.

And what that key unlocks we cannot know:
prison or garden, man must make it so. The mole
lacks vision to distinguish, and is jailed
beneath the rosebush. There's security.

And I must climb, to set my grandchild free.

Choice

This life is hard, and full of woe,
    its pitfalls deep;
a truth that any bard may know
    who troubles sleep.

We dig our holes till time must stop,
    then find them steep;
or crop our souls to sow our crop,
    which others reap.

We pile up dirt from side to side
    and upward creep,
which brings us hurt when down we slide
    all in a heap.

To gather me dung from here to damn
    makes life seem cheap;
I'd rather be hung for the Lamb
    than a sheep.

Civil Defense

When the just God presents at last his bill
for services unrendered: must we fall
abjectly to the gutter? crawl
on unrepentant knees to crouch beneath the sill?
assume the posture science dictates? drill
will now to cringe, force flesh to improvise
that fœtal twisting where alone salvation lies?
wait, warned and bewardened, willing for the kill?

Let me meet six-feet-under six feet tall:
the prophet heard no word from heaven until
he rose at its command. With bump and bawl
we learned to stand; shall we not stand then still?
... When the last vast mushroom fills the skies,
stand up. Let God see the whites of your eyes.

Lines for the Dedication
of a Fallout Shelter

Put not your trust in princes: Nick nor Jack
nor any man commands such megatons to drown
your last betrayal: Gabriel, old clown,
has crowed you twice already. Turn you back
and render: there's a mortgage on this shack
no Cæsar's coin will tender. Take you down
the rubbled byways of your silent town
to die a man beside the twisted track
your fathers jumped. And stop along the way
to do some stupid, honest kindness to a cow,
a flower, or a misplaced stone (if man
survives, he is beyond you). Did you plan
to live forever? Do it now.
And Nick nor Jack nor I can say you nay.

Ninth Hour

Now all is policy: our generals
have learned to coo like doting fathers, which,
undoubtedly, they are. Anxious to prove
their manhood, refugees arrive
from shady universities. How to do the job
becomes the burning question of the hour.
It is too late for answers. Even if
we knew, we have no time.

Remembering Lot's uncertain wife, we plunge
into the jungle: who will buy
our violets? The market is unsteady; few reply.
Who'll take this flower? Silence. Gently, then,
these petals on this grave. We shall adopt
all orphans under military age.

This man has touched no food in fifty days;
we marvel at his tiresome constancy. St. Jude,
uphold him, lest his body turn to salt
from such inversion of established ways:
war, breakfast, struggle, orphans, lunch.
Logistics form the pattern of our time:
crawl forward, eat at stated hours, toss
grenades at intervals. Hail, Cæsars, we
who are about to die support you: see,
our carpenters have finished with the cross.

Letter to an American Advisor

Defender of the Freedoms, hail. Your deeds
are known to us: the village, loyal (or,
at least, protected); war
up to the gates; and one small boy who needs
companionship. You offer him a bar
of GI chocolate. His father (Oriental, sly)
hides with the other men; he wonders why,
and takes another candy: "*There* the tunnels are."

What have we gained, Defender, now
that tunnels, fathers, chocolates are done?
A Mars bar's worth of ribbons in the line
of duty, to amuse your sweet-toothed son
back home? And will you tell him how?
And how (one question more) shall I tell mine?

God Will Be a Little Late This Year

THIS STABLE BEING OCCUPIED, BY TROOPS
OF THIS OR THAT PERSUASION, AND THE CRIB
BEING REQUISITIONED AS A STORAGE-BIN
FOR GEAR OF UNKNOWN MANUFACTURE, LIB-
ERTY TO STOP BY THIS CONVENIENT INN
IS STRINGENTLY CURTAILED; ALL GROUPS,
EXCEPT OF DULY-NOTED PERSONNEL,
ARE SUSPECT, AND ARE APT TO BE ATTACKED;
NO FACTS MAY BE REVEALED OF OUR EXACT
LOCATION, BUT WE ARE NOT FAR FROM HELL.

yet history, even here, assumes in part
the classic stance: here baffled wisemen seek,
and poor men guard their fields, and herods speak
in varied accents and unvarying tones;
the cities gulp the frantic and afraid;
the hills and valleys choke themselves on bones;
here man has reached an end, and who shall start
love's penetration of hate's barricade?

rejected, cornered, outcast, born in strife . . .
what Child is this who crashes through to life?

Four Poems for Advent

I

The drugstore blares the tunes of Christmas day:
now Mama kisses Santa, Christ is born,
in happy alternation. Clerks look worn
(as does the merchandise). Across the way
an organ swells the sales of high-priced stock
where weary shoppers chat their way through Bach.
Late-comers crowd the inns to park their toasts
in some dim corner by the pinball games.
Salvation's saints, and Jesus' jangling dames,
strategically spotted on the edge of time,
tinkle incessant bells like Marley's scrawny ghosts,
or like bored judges in a traffic-mill
reminding us that God, too, sends a bill.
And on the 26th the windows of the local five-and-dime
entreat us all to buy a Valentine.

II

Three days till Childermas: the celebration
means little to the modern, democratic nation.
Herod is obsolete: our innocents
slaughter themselves; with childish violence
bend twig and trigger against future fate,
or spit their brothers on the sword of state.

Homeward, the wise men took another path, but we
still circle round the gifts beneath the tree,
hoping that corporate ingenuity extends
sufficient love to little citizens.
This day the childish heart is king and queen,
and mayhem grows in gadgets on the evergreen.

Postpone the mourning: there's a savior born
each moment as the tinsel wrapping's torn.
Joy fill his day, no sobs disturb his sleep:
when Rachel mothers Cain, for whom shall Rachel weep?

III

Having broken the rock and beheld water;
having broken the stone and beheld the anger of God;
having led ourselves into the desert, farther
than ever Israelite trod:

We pause. Reflect. Water is not in this land.
There is no wind. The eastern star has set.
Routine plods forward, but the end —
the end is not yet.

Lord, in this year of the burning sun
of the desert, of vultures and sand:
let that star shine on us again;
show us the Land.

As on the second mountain Moses,
breaker of tablets, giver of the law,
dying, forbidden entry, still with joyous eyes
the promise saw.

May also unto us the Child be given,
that to our hate-worn hearts He may bequeath
the power to plod on, though far from heaven,
and hope and faith.

IV

All this can be explained: the Child, the star,
the Eastern sages, and King Herod's spleen,
the credulous shepherds with their angel choir,
the tinsel trappings of the manger scene.

Logic refutes this documentary air:
these prophecies were made to fit the fact;
symbolic purposes are all too clear,
and royal lineage is, obviously, stacked.

Yet still we kneel. Reality is not
mere conjugation of the kicked-at stone
(this too shall roll away). Now God is known,
impending, not to be evaded, caught
by time, flesh, passion, pain, death, will,
and on that birth the stars are singing still.

Brief Pause for Station Identification

then the mariners were afraid,
and cried each unto his own god

How silently the hour hand falls beneath
the shadow of its longer, quicker self:
invisible, it signals from the quiet shelf
the hour of breaking bread, and drawing breath.
Muted, the frantic presses grant a moment's grace
to some doomed, giant spruce a thousand miles away,
and idly scorn poor flesh, that must betray
a hungry culture from their automatic pace.

The silent moment passes: from atop the city hall
raucous officialdom now ratifies the hour,
asserts the greatest good within its power:
the air-raid horn lets out its daily bawl
(throaty, obscene, and violent) to notify
the clockless voter of his time of rest,
and comfort the compact majority who nest
invincibly defended from the sky.

The militant, recorded church disputes the air:
from equal height and power, harmonious and bland,
the chimes of Trinity (Reformed) now take their stand
beneath the cross of Jesus — whose electric prayer
recalls an earlier world turned upside-down.
Eternity now dangles from this gilt-edged spire,

delivering time and revolutions, and by wire
the cultured chimes console the modern town.

The neighbor's dog exerts his democratic right
to challenge the authority that gives him pain:
he hurls his howls toward hall and heaven, in vain —
against the creature church and state unite.
Fair science sings the now secure, the future blest,
and flesh must yield to these unconscious powers
that have no ears to hear, but keep their towers
and leave his pleas ignored, his grievance unredressed.

And I, assaulted by this trinity of noise,
retire to my appointed corner, lunch
on three wax-papered sandwiches, the usual bunch
of supermarket grapes.
                              The clock destroys
my silence; presses gulp; the far-off tree
topples. An empty lunch-box rattles out my worth,
crying, to all who snap the switches of this earth:
this is my body, broken every day for thee.

Destination Hell

Having loused up one planet beyond all redemption,
we progress: Mars, Venus, the moon, platforms in space —
with man all things are possible, except to face
the probability he nowhere gains exemption
from the irredeemable laws of consequence, whence
we flee, jet-powered, helmeted, armored against fate,
the universe, and God. (Creatures of any other state
assumed unfriendly by the logic of our own events.)

Is there no balm in Pleiad? are no quiet skies
reserved for mind to lodge at while an old world melts?
Now David's smallest grandson, goat of cattle cars,
with idle finger flicks the globe and tries
the classic shrug: "But have you nothing else?"
This question begs no answer. Villains, give us back our stars.

No

Freedom is less than a word: it need not speak
when truth is silence, and the marketplace is filled
with voices. Freedom must be willed
in the shattering stubborn stillness of the meek.

Freedom is never affirmed: it may be named
only in its denial; weaponless, it fights;
commands allegiance, yet confers no rights;
can live by firesides, but is never tamed.

Freedom can never be bought, though often sold
and advertised at discounts; must be paid
with interest, on demand; adds to no trade;
it has no price but cost; has weight, but not in gold.

Freedom may never be held: rots in deep-freeze;
like Baucis' pitcher, freedom must be poured
out to the bottom; is its own reward;
rests on its feet, because it has no knees.

Sonnet for Solo Violin

Up betimes: the city stricken with a plague
(and fire to follow). Luncheon with milord,
the week's provisions to be bought and stored,
the rents collected, several bills unpaid
(apply to have the interest rates reduced),
the carriage wants repairs, a new report
due at the coming session of the court,
milady's latest chambermaid still unseduced.

So the world's work goes on, through fires or floods,
wars, famines, even Gabriel's final toot
will find this fiddling antheap drags along
the greatest number of the greatest goods.
...Ah, Nero, Nero, why such ill repute?
at least you marked your city's downfall with a song.

Unheard Cassandra

Greeks, beware of gifts: these loaves
accompany no miraculous fishes,
enfold no files, no hacksaw blades —
only a promissory note for bank-night dishes,
the usual shells and beads, a few grenades,
electric lighting for Olympian groves.

Run to the shore. Like Priam putting on
victorious robes admit the conqueror
who hides within; nor heed the captive's call,
"gods' mills grind slowly bitter bread." Once more
Thucydides remarks the city's fall,
strange chevrons gleaming in the Parthenon.

Collage

one whitewashed room: three thousand turned away;
the blued nudes nuzzle canvas; beer
invades the fuel tanks; something smells on tape.

                          wheels turn:
the library piano burns; the governor
has been invited: isn't that?

                          birds die:
some weep; some laugh (i understand);
                         this way
to the egress:
                    it is the end, one cheerful said,
                    who will be (when he dead is) dead.

The Construction Project

That immortality devised by finite minds,
that rears up pyramids on Egypt's sands,
names peaks and rivers, fills booksellers' stands,
and scrawls initials on the highway signs

must bear the guilt. On Shinar's plain
a conference of the elders of the earth
engaged an architect (which marks the birth
of science, logic, and the bulging brain),

held competition for the finest engineer,
and set the masses to the kiln. With slime
and brick they sought to wall out time,
and build a tomb against the social fear:

that history might not even realize
they had existed. (This is not to be
admitted. Civilized society
demands at least a footnote; so arise

our towers, course on course.) This one progressed:
the scaffolds being sound, the masons quick,
inspectors having passed on every brick,
and science having mastered every test.

Now Shinar's plain resounds to violins
rehearsing, and the orators and choirs,

and kindergarteners dancing to the lyres.
The patriarch accepts the golden trowel, and begins

to lay the final mortar. Consternation.
Enter the villain of this intellectual scene:
God. Scatters the audience in a fit of spleen
at having been an object of invasion;

pronounces judgment like a movie tough:
"You know too much. When you know all,
consider, man, how far you'll have to fall";
and wipes another culture off the cuff.

Now down come patriarch, bricks, mortar, crowd,
ambition, golden trowel, even hod.
Nothing, save dust, ascends. Since which time God
is worshipped (as He should be) in a cloud.

The Mortician

The flowers are very tastefully arranged. The mourners
approach by twos and threes the door, which swings
discreetly open, having recently been oiled. Such things
as might offend the sensitive are hid in corners.
The hushed tones match the suit exactly: "Would you care
to view the body?" (Craftsman's pride
in job well done.) The glove to guide,
the sadly reassuring smile, the chair
for each potential ultimate consumer. Not unnerved
by grief or details, has each necessary car,
each driver, and God's spokesman at his post,
and cues them in on time. And is death served
by these obsequious obsequies? And is our cross no bar
to some sad silent meeting with his ghost?

Eugenics for the Masses

The learnèd phrenologist, with his Bump of Love
displaced by newer knowledge, now attacks
the wonders of creation. Dietary lacks,
prenatal trauma, and the errors of
the vagrant sperm, the uninstructed gene,
are measured, microscoped, statisticized, and seen
as monstrous flaws of nature, not to be endured
when surgeons could prevent what can't be cured.

Who will define the monster, monster? Once these fools
outranked you in kings' palaces, and spoke
the simple truths that wiser men would choke
(and gag on still), and all the sideshow tools
of God, the dwarf and giant, had their place:
reminders of the mystery of grace.
Blest then be God, and let His handwork be:
"Who variest the forms of His creation" — even thee.

Salute to an Honest Confectioner

This happy chocolate bunny, perched astride
his chocolate rocket missile, adds a clever touch.
(I never thought the plain ones looked like much,
and as for Easter eggs and yellow chicks and such,
they're clearly dated, like the virgin bride
atop the wedding cake.)   One recalls with pride
the giant, gaily-colored metal eggs
our gallant airmen dropped to celebrate this day
a few short years ago — a forceful way
to proselyte.   There's progress, I should say,
and now this cosmic rabbit smiles and begs
acceptance of the symbol tucked between his legs:
now power is fertility, the limit is the sky,
the gods are on the shelf for all to buy.

Marshmallow crosses add a somber note, arrayed
among the jelly beans; coated in black
(but never bitter) chocolate, they attack
uneasy memories of faith gone slack
amid the fleshpots; yet be not dismayed:
the shock technique, researchers prove, has always paid,
and these drab sweets will sell, to fill an empty nook
in many an Easter basket.   Here once more
symbol has conquered meaning in their private war:
what can't be comprehended can be purchased at the store.
But what would Pilate say, could he but look
at crosses made of goosh, besmeared with guck?
... Who chews this ten-cent totem yet may find
a diabetic heaven, and peace of mind.

Never a Spray of Yew

Desked among the portraits of the great and the elected
you lunched for the photographer on a glass of milk
                                        and an apple,
facing fame and annihilation with the same cautious sobriety.
(Now you appraise me, calmly, from an upper corner
of Yuletide Greetings, letters from my son, the plumber's bill.)

Calvin's last gentleman, Wall Street's predestined gift
                                        to the atom,
you divided worlds like apples with the carefree morality
of a mediæval pope.
                    Already the body,
feeding, turned in upon itself, mirroring the mind
that could play at war with surgical symbols,
and knew only two classes: the Evil Men
and Us.

            How did it feel, statesman, when the pain
forced itself at the last on your attention,
achieving a momentary triumph beyond the power
of Bantu, Catalan, or fellaheen? When they shook their heads
and ordered morphine, did you halt
(the untasted fruit gone bitter in the mind)
at the brink of some uncertain, undefended disaster?

Or did you whistle for a missile to roll back
the dark light of your final, private defeat? Were we to be
your last retaliation? Foster, enemy and friend,
repentance needs no protocol.

The Time Is Now Standard

(October 27, 1962)

The crisis has now, we are officially informed, officially ended,
and we turn back the clock an hour earlier
than we had intended;
Republicans and Russians are once more defeated
(they will return) and our depleted
nerves, accepting yet another hour, must soon prepare to rise
to another day, another time,
another carefully prepared surprise.

What have we learned? (aside from the obvious facts
that Chase & Sanborn's has the flavor, Total lacks
no vitamins, tobacco has abolished cancer) —
who ask for news tonight receive the same old answer:
our weapons are defensive, theirs are not;
we must be strong to keep what we have got.

It works. The New Frontier maintains the ancient barriers
with firmness, submarines, and aircraft carriers;
Monroe applauds; Dutch-uncled with a Harvard intonation,
the enemy withdraws its battle-station.

Pundits advise unanimous consent; at worst,
an egg or two: the tiny campus handfuls are dispersed,
upholding their statistics. We relax,
and turn again to football or the income tax
as, slowly on a hill in Palestine,
new blood drips down
(like Mogen David wine

The Tragedy at Prinknash Abbey

I

Leslie Dally, one fall day,
at Prinknash Abbey earned his pay
raking orchard leaves away.

A gardener by social station,
he long had held his situation
and did his work by automation
dreaming of next year's brief vacation;

yet never failed to give his best
to horticulture's every test
despite his name (a hairy vest)
that prompted many a cleric jest,
and set him off from all the rest.

Meanwhile, from an apple's crown,
Brother Christopher looked down
upon the landscape sere and brown.

The fruit was gone, the boughs were bare,
there was no hiding place up there;
the sun was cold, and cold the air —
it hardly seemed a place for prayer.

Why should the monk have climbed the tree?
a question not for such as we.
Perhaps a penance, or a spree?

Perhaps he merely wished to see
across the wall, two miles or three?

Perhaps he thought himself well hid
to spy out whether Dally did?
Perhaps at Prinknash climbing forms
no deviation from the norms,
and birds' nests gathered for indulgence
emit miraculous effulgence?

Could he have hoped to turn back time
and stop Eve's hand by words sublime?
arrest the fall 'round Newton's ears,
and reinstate the seven spheres?
or, just by climbing *up* the tree,
refute the law of gravity?

Or did he hope to meet his Lord?
History does not record.

Now Fate stepped in, with leaden tread,
and Furies gathered overhead:
Dally, pursuing errant leaves,
halted to button up his sleeves
beneath the tree where sat the brother
(would God that he had picked another!),

at which precise historic time,
predestined from primordial slime,

the most high churchman lost his grip
and took a most uncleric flip;
obeying Newton, after all,
found Adam not the last to fall;
yet would have gone to heaven, I know,
had not poor Dally been below.

The gardener, who could not prepare
for heavenly bodies from the air,
found Christopher too much to bear,

sustained a most ungodly whack,
and perished, of a broken back.

II

The gardener he stood by an apple-tree trunk,
    (heigh-ho, says Dally)
when all of a sudden he met with a monk.
    (with a rally, Dally, sally and rally,
    heigh-ho, says Leslie and Dally)

The monk came a-hurrying down from the tree,
    (heigh-ho, the abbey)
which made of poor Dally a sight for to see.
    (with an abbey crabbie, scabby and grabby,
    heigh-ho, says Prinknash and Abbey)

The monk gave the gardener a blow on the spine
    (heigh-ho, the apple)
from which Leslie Dally did ever repine.
    (with a dapple apple, pratfall and scrapple,
    heigh-ho, the fall of the apple)

The point of my story it's plain for to see:
    (heigh-ho, now wine us and dine us)
THE MONK SHOULD HAVE NEVER COME DOWN FROM THE TREE.
    (singing ipso facto, arris and tottle,
    Q. E. D., *says thomas aquinas)*

III

In Adam's fall we sinnèd all
    and fell from holy station;
in sweat and dread to earn our bread,
    awaiting our salvation.

While bitter fruit on Newton's snoot
    established gravitation
by falling raw into his law,
    and outlawed levitation.

From Adam's fa' and Newton's law
    may Christ our Lord defend us:
loose feet from sod, turn minds to God,
    whose grace alone can mend us.

A Question of Gravity

Plaything of all that moves, this bouncing earth
must rise to meet each new invading force:
exploding suns conspire against its course,
and passing comets slyly test its worth
(it gives a little when you shake it); rain
may make a difference, too, and falling tears,
or soldiers dropping.   Engineers
lack instruments to seismograph the pain
our battered, reeling globe sustains from all
the tuggings of creation (as their tools
approach precision, one child's rubber ball
may throw the calculus askew).
                              Who rules
this shaky orbit knows how long, how far
earth yet must leap to greet the Christmas star.

A Cross for Christmas

Wisdom begins in a far-off land
and rides a bumpy steed;
humility is near at hand
with sheep to feed.

Wisdom surveys uncharted ways
and ponders paths that part;
humility reads across the maze
the map within the heart.

Wisdom tunes exhausted ears
on scholar, priest, and king;
humility in silence hears
the word the angels bring.

Wisdom deploys a caravan
against the darkening night;
humility lacks a private plan
and travels light.

Where love is born our paths begin
that vanished in its loss;
the straightest line from God to men
leads to a cross.

Who'd presents bring to Christ the king
may neither stop nor sleep;
who'd hear the song his angels sing
must tend his sheep.

Reprise for Lewis Carroll

"It is wrong," said the caterpillar sternly,
"from beginning to end."

Could you return, old Logicker, you'd write
Victorian romance.   Your pawns would be
mere pieces in a game, of ivory
(not flesh of peasant, skewered left and right);
Tweedles, if fight they would, would crowless fight
in purely private quarrels; jabberwock you'd free
for childhood's secret language (we'd agree
to shelter it from governments); white knight,
red king would tip no board nor order; grins
would vanish after politicians, leaving cats;
the walrus would go hungry, and the dormouse pass
from Nam to Cong, or Congo, selling hats.
Then, having done your tale that each man wins,
you'd call it (darkly) *Through the Looking Glass.*

And Smog

While I agree about the fire
(also the ice),
I fear our world may not require
desire or hate or other vice
so violent to cause its fate.

For there's a smog we all inspire
that insulates us from desire
or from, indifferently, hate.

Fact is, our world could perish thrice
just being nice.

Quarry, What Huntsman?

Fleeing the four-wheeled proletarians, at last he came
to a hillside of suspicious snakes, and nervous bees
(none of the fauna could be classified as tame):
good-will was mostly thumbs, and would not do;
the broccoli grew lice and died, the snow-topped trees
blew down his birthday, and battered a hole in the view.

Happy the man who builds his home on rock, and earns
the gift of contemplation, even undesired;
only his back is practical, though politics returns,
having buttered no boulders, to shim the crooked doors;
his field is history, given as required
(as, centipedes are fond of concrete floors).

Bearing the scars of the builder, he must now confront
the doctrines of construction: he who calls the tune
must pay the piper; easy dogmas blunt
like poorly-sharpened chisels on a knot;
bent nails make heavy hammers; all too soon
the rains remember what he had forgot.

The act of faith is mainly concrete: sand
can (in the aggregate) provide
routine stability, but will not stand
beyond the working of the lime of time

that powders all to dust, and will deride
the subdivision and the urbane rhyme.

His home now hugs the hills, although they hide
dayspring and life's end, the extemporizing seasons,
makeshift and maintenance and moment. Cast aside,
old blueprints lose their glamor under dust;
and each new wall has cornered him with reasons
to start from rock, as every builder must.

Notes

"How Silently, How Silently..." — This poem owes a great deal to Donald M. Baillie's book, *God Was in Christ.*

"Variations on a Theme by John Donne" — The quotation is from Stanza VII, "The Patriarchs," of *A Litany.*

"The Window" — The quotation is from *A Vision of the Last Judgment.*

"Can These Bones Live?" — The first sentence represents my apprehension of George Fox's probable reaction on a visit to most of our contemporary Quaker meetings, but the poem as a whole will be cheerfully shared with any religious group that can find itself a rhyme for the first line.

"For Wilmer Young" — Wilmer J. Young, Quaker educator and social pioneer, was convicted in 1959 in U. S. District Court for his part in the "Omaha Action" demonstration against the construction of the first intercontinental ballistic missile launching base. This poem was inspired by his statement to the court.

"Lines for the Dedication of a Fallout Shelter" — written during the Krushchev-Kennedy era, hence "Nick nor Jack."

"Ninth Hour" — "This man" is Lee Stern, who engaged in a lengthy fast in protest against the initial escalation of the Vietnam war in 1965. "Letter to an American Advisor" is based on a *New York Times* dispatch from the period when such activity was considered a brilliant stroke of "counter-insurgency." "God Will Be a Little Late This Year" was reprinted in the Borestone Mountain *Best Poems of 1966,* in which I shared with the always-reliable Denise Levertov the distinction of knowing there was a war on.

"Brief Pause for Station Identification" — The quotation at the head of the poem is from Jonah 1:5.

Notes

"Destination Hell" — The joke on which the sestet is based dates back only, so far as I can determine, to the Nazi period; however it seems to me an outstanding example of classic Jewish humor. The final sentence is taken from the banner of the French peasants who marched on Robespierre's Paris, armed with rakes and scythes: "Villains, give us back our God."

"Unheard Cassandra" — This poem was written several years before Radio Corporation of America had informed an admiring nation, through full-page, tax-deductible advertisements, of its electronic achievements on Mount Ida. No occult powers are claimed; it was inevitable.

"Eugenics for the Masses" — The quotation is from a prayer to be offered "on seeing strangely formed persons, such as giants or dwarfs" (Hebrew Prayer Book).

"Salute to an Honest Confectioner" — This poem is dedicated to my neighbor, the sculptor Aleko Kyriakos, who used to keep body and soul together by designing Easter candies (but never marshmallow crosses).

"The Tragedy at Prinknash Abbey" — based on a UPI dispatch from Gloucester in 1962, which included the names of the two central characters. Some years after writing this poem I learned from an English friend that the proper pronunciation is "Prinnich Abbey." This does not seem to alter the sound of the poem from the way I wrote it, but I do regret having lost the chance of a lifetime to get a rhyme for "spinach." I am totally unable to explain the coincidence that "rowley, powley, gammon, etc.," got in there anyhow.